Introduction:

It's very true! Yes, you can make over six figures plus a year Web Camming, Part time or Full time. With this guide you will be able to know and understand all the requirements, time and techniques to make or keep yourself debt free and enjoy the finer things in life, by being your boss and sticking to a consistent schedule. It would give you more time to spend with family and travel the world. Now who wouldn't want that? Web Camming can be for everyone because there's always someone for everyone. Thick, Skinny, BBW, Men, Trans there is no discrimination. Even the elders are Web Camming getting to the (Bag!) virtually. Privacy features allow you to block regions, helping to eliminate the chance of someone you know seeing you performing on cam. DMCA is the process of getting copyrighted content removed from the internet. If you find any stolen webcam shows, contact support and the company will send out the takedown requests on your behalf. Geo-blocking capability allows you to block any country, state or city. If you are a US model, you can block your home state as well as any state you have ever lived in. If you are outside of the United States, you can block your home country and only appear in countries outside of where you live. Be apart of new innovations and a Comfortable/Safe way to work from anywhere in the world with a laptop or cell phone. Make your everyday routine entertaining for your fans. If it's (Cooking, Sexy Fitness Fetish, Foot Fetish, Balloon Popping, Gigantes Fetish, Lipstick Fetish, Financial Domination, Virtual Movie Night to name a few of the very broad arena. As you continue with these Sections, understand that your end results can or will change your life. Only you can stand in your way.

        Be Great, Be Entertaining,

        Be Consistent, Be a Boss

Getting Started

If you have your requirements checked off, let's get started! Sign up to the Web Cam Site of your choice below are a few top sites.

1. Myfreecams.com pays 50%

2.Streamatemodels.com pays 35%

3.Camsoda.com pays 50%

4. Badgirlent.com pays 50%

Now these are just the top sites I recommend and yes 35% from Streamate it's sounds horrible compared to the other sites, but Streamate is one of the largest networks on the web they have over 700 websites domains. You can definitely make a lot of money with them and not recognize your receiving 35% because of the huge traffic flow that you're always receiving. There are still thousands of dollars to be made each week with Streamate. They are the leader in the Web Cam industry but Myfreecams is the main sponsor for the AVN awards and Exxotica and other main adult events. So, they carry a heavy name as well. The great thing about Myfreecams is that they allow you to cross market such as advertising your personal website or anything that you're doing in the industry that you want people to be aware about, it's an excellent way to promote yourself on a huge network for free and still make money out of it. Camsoda is a little bit like Myfreecams they provide marketing and they let you cross market to advertise your Instagram, Twitter, Snapchat and so forth. Camsoda and Myfreecams are also more of tipping sites, Streamate is more of a private site, in free chat certain things are limited. No nudity except if you like to accept tips for a sexy breast tease or pose in a thong or sexy boy shorts. Streamate also has a Non-Nude model section for Sign up. There's something for everyone once again. Myfreecams and Camsoda anything goes in free chat, these sites are really based on tipping. Streamate you can never cross market that is a huge no-no, don't ever do that or they will ban your account, where you can't

work and that's one account and you

don't want to lose since they are the

King of Web Cam. It's always a guarantee you

will make money with Streamate. Select which

Site or Sites would be better for you. Study the

models, go into the chat rooms observe and

view different niches and check out the

couples chat. Couples chat rooms make

a lot of money if you have a boyfriend or

girlfriend that might be interested in

working with you, getting paid all day

to be with the love of your life or close

friend intimately and having an entertaining

time streaming from the comfortability of

your home or wherever your streaming journey takes you. "It's a huge moneymaker". The male or female talent must sign up same as you did or are doing, and they will connect the account as a couple account. Here are some additional sites that have been around for a long time that are Trustworthy and Reliable. But not as active as the previous Webcam Sites listed above. Most of these sites listed below provide the model with mobile streaming ability. Which is a big deal and a huge benefit.

* Cam4.com Pays 50%

* Herbicepscam. com Pays 50%

* Pinkcams.com Pays 50%

* IFriends.com Pays 50%+

* Imlive.com Pays 50%

* Livejasmin.com Pays 50% +

Take some time but not too much and do some research, watch the live models streaming cams and just feel the vibe and understand how the system works from the outsiders / fans perspective. All model sign ups require a Valid ID, Driver's license or Passport. And a Headshot. The ID must be held next to your face about right next to your cheek. Make sure, it is a clear photo and if you zoom in you can see the ID information clearly so, when it is time for approval you will get a approved and not denied. If you're into cosplay, that type of content can perform very well. Especially if you're very good at cosplay. Having a wide range of costumes and other outfits allows for different type of role-playing and can help to increase the diversity of your content and target different fetishes and niches.

It never hurts to have a lovely toy chest aside. If you already have a large collection, perfect. If not, it is something that you can build up over time. It is also a good idea to keep a Wishlist and add all the toys you want as Wishlist items. Adult stars often

get spoiled by their fans Via: Wishlist. This is a great way to build up your toy collection without investing a single penny. A great Wishlist site to sign up on is Deliverycode.com once the order is placed by your fans they cannot cancel it and your gift is on its way. Everything is discreet and protected for your mailing purposes. Unlike Amazon they can cancel your gift after the order is placed.
So deliverycode.com protects you and your gifts. No Indian givers allowed!

Section1: Requirements

Let's get started on some of the main equipment you would need for a successful business in the Web Camming Industry.

1. Laptop with a fast Processor
2. HD/ 4K Webcam (Logitech) recommended
3. Lightning Internet Speed
4. Great Lighting

Individual Information required for Webcam sign up. Must be 18 years and older and have Valid Identification. It would take about 2 to 3 days on some Webcam sites for approval, in some instance's approval can be within 24 hours.

Once approved you can start working immediately and bringing in that check.

A 3-point lighting system is a great investment. You can buy the lighting system, create your own inexpensively.

If you're not shooting in a place with good natural (or artificial) light, a 3-point lighting system is a must! Going from bad lighting to good lighting is the single easiest ways to increase the quality of your live stream. Not having good lighting is also a very common mistake of beginner models and producers. Find a nice comfortable creative space where you would be able to set up your Web Cam area.

Decorative lighting, Plush pillows or even an Office set up. Be the boss at work who everyone fantasizes about good or bad. *20 shades of Grey*........ You create your Web Cam show how you want to, What's your forte? Don't think that there won't be anybody interested in watching you do the laundry, polish your toes even eat a large meal. There are so many fetishes out there it's unbelievable believable, select the niche that is comfortable for you and you will always be successful in this industry. Further in this guide you will be provided with popular Niches, Online times to work, and the Top Web

Cam Sites to sign up with. Some sites pay Bi- Monthly, a lot pay Weekly and very few let you cash out Daily. Work multiple sites if you like, not streaming at the same time because it will slow down your live stream, but if you super highspeed internet working off separate computers and streaming simultaneously can be accomplished if certain sites allow that. (Check their Rules and Guidelines). And if so, bring in that "Double Check". Set your hours for sites and bring in Double or Triple the cash. This is the Manifesto of The Web Cam Internet Modeling Industry, grab a highlighter, keep notes of "Key Items" for your daily consistency in this evolving network.

Section 2: Your Approved!

Congratulations! You are now ready to begin and enjoy a stress-free lifestyle change. Be the Boss you were destined to be. Now hopefully you have taken the time out to study the industry. Now that you are approved, order some sexy attire or whatever makes you comfortable for live cam, order items for your newfound business at a great discount particularly for Adult Entertainers. If you selected to join a cam site that allows you to cross market. The next step is to create a Twitter particularly in relation to whatever stage name you decided to use. Twitter is a huge promotional site especially in relation to adult entertainment.

Instagram is another helpful platform, but Twitter comes first for this industry. So just make sure you keep your stage name in sync for the new accounts you create. Promote and brand yourself. Just like anything it takes time to build up "The Brand" but not that long. With social networking promotion and the huge networks that are already working for you, in a month you will have over hundreds of fans or more. Now you should have some start up items and you have a nice creative space to work out of, now you are ready to log on. But let's understand the best times to log on and make the most of your time. It's always great to complete a total of 8 hours minimum, and a wonderful method is breaking it up into 2-hour increments. Below listed are the best times to work. You will eventually get a feel for your personal times that work best.

Starting Work Week:

Sunday:

8:00am- 9:00am   12:00pm-3:00pm
6:00pm- 8:00pm
10:00pm-12:00am

Monday:

6:30am- 10:30am 12:00pm- 1:30pm
5:00pm- 8:00pm
10:00pm-12:00am

Tuesday:

6:30am- 10:30am   1:00pm - 3:00pm
5:00pm - 8:00pm 10:00pm - 12:00am

Wednesday:

7:00am - 10:00am 12:30pm - 1:30pm
4:00pm - 8:00pm 10:00pm – 12:00am

Thursday:

7:00am - 10:00am
12:30pm - 1:30pm   4:00pm - 8:00pm
10:00pm - 12:00am

Friday:

7:00am - 10:00am
11:00am - 2:00pm 5:00pm - 8:00pm
10:00pm - 1:00am   3:30am - 4:30am

Saturday:

7:00am - 9:00am
10:30am - 8:00pm 1 0:00pm - 2:00am

Keep in mind your fans have families, executive jobs and more. And they still make time for their webcam models. They want to know your happy and satisfied. They love to know how your day went and what trip your taking next on their expense. They love to join you on a virtual movie night, or in the kitchen cooking up something delicious. Create an experience that's comfortable and beneficial for you and entertaining for them. The important things to know and remember. Always speak and type. Acknowledge a Tip and say, "Thank You". Shout them out for a moment which will turn them into a fan and start building your numbers and your online status for moving your brand forward to front page of the site you are modeling on. If you encounter rudeness don't blow the rooms vibe. Just hit that block button and continue with the entertainment. It's not worth having an attitude from one person's ignorance and loosing tips from another. Keep great energy in your chat room and make it rememberable. There are so many fetishes in this world. I wanted to provide you with some of the top fetishes that may fall in your category that you were not aware about.

Top Fetishes

*Financial Domination *Findom*Adult Role Play*

Giantess / Gigantess

* Goddess Worship

*Foot Fetish*Amateur*Arm Pitt Fetish

*Ass Fetish*Ass Worship

*Ball busting*Balloon Popping *BBC

*BBW*BDSM*Belly Fetish*Bikini

*Blackmail Fetish *Blackmail Fantasy

*Blonde Goddess

*Blowjob*Body Worship*Boot Domination *Boot Fetish*Brat Girls

*Burping*Chastity*Coerced Bi*Cosplay*Cream pie*Cuckold

*Cum Countdown

*Cum Eating Instructions (CEI)*Dirty Feet* Talk *Domination*Eating*Edging*Farting* Female Wrestling *Femdom* Findom *Glove Fetish*Hand jobs*High Heels*Home Wrecker *Housewife.

With all this detailed information now it's time for you to take control, keep a schedule, keep a positive outlook and keep that check coming in with Daily, Weekly and Bi-Weekly pay.

In this section there is a breakdown of how much you can make Daily, Weekly, Monthly and Yearly. It's very easy to achieve these numbers with consistency. The numbers listed below are based upon a 7-day work week.

	Daily	Weekly	Monthly	Yearly
1.	*$150	$1050	$4200	$50,400
2.	*$200	$1400	$5600	$67,200
3.	*$250	$1750	$7000	$84,000
4.	*$300	$2100	$8400	$100,800
5.	*$350	$2450	$9800	$117,600
6.	*$400	$2800	$11,200	$134,400
7.	*$450	$3150	$12,600	$151,200
8.	*$500	$3500	$14,000	$168,000

Deposits can be Check by mail, ACH, Paxum, Wire Transfer and few more that the sites will inform you of. There is an ability to put your payments on hold also if you like to hit a certain goal or if you're in the process of any changes. The hold can be lifted at any time. Any payments will resume as usual. If you are planning on making this your mainstream income. Keep in mind that you will be building a brand. Once you get the hang of it, purchase a domain name and create a subscription website to bring in more residual

revenue.

Use the Url:
http://www.Tiffaniloveclub.com/signup
to set up your *"Free"* website, which you will be able to Live Stream, Receive Tips, Upload Videos,

Pictures, Schedule Appearance Dates and receive Wishlist gifts. Which all will bring in additional revenue and commerce. Make sure you always put aside funds for emergencies or just save, save, save to buy that dream home, purchase that new piece of property, purchase that dream car or Travel Around the World. With any of the webcam companies you are considered a self employed
1099 model. Therefore, you will file your taxes as independent contractor.

You are the Boss!

Important Tips When Live Streaming

1. Always have a positive attitude.

2. Speak to your fans.

3. Don't forget to Type, some fans may be at work or elsewhere and the model is on
"Mute" on their end. Typing is always important.

4. Don't let other irrelevant people ruin your vibe. Just "BLOCK" them.

5. Have great lighting.

6. Create an atmosphere or go to a legal area where you can Live Stream and Entertain. (Car, Backyard, Park, Kitchen, Office, Home Gym, Private Beach etc.)

7. Use Props: (Eyeglasses, Fruit, Lotion, Oil, Bubble

Gum, Lollipops,

Adult Novelty, Stockings, Whips, Paddles, Balloons etc.)

8. Anime & Role-play is very popular so if you're into dressing up. Keep Lingerie and
Anime Outfits updated and ready at hand. Also, Card games and Cooking shows are
very popular.

9. There is a note section, so once you attain your fans, keep track of their name and what they are into etc. Most of the Cam Sites you can click on the member name and "Note" section will pop up. It makes it easier and more intimate, the next time the member arrives back into your cam room and you welcome them by their name or by knowing what they like. It increases your "Tip "and "Private Chat "chances because your "Fan" is comfortable now; they love the feeling you know them personally in such a way.

10. Don't break the rules to sites. Abide by each.

11. Have fun and make lots of money!

Section 5: 70 Positive Affirmations

Ego worries will never make you more money. Therefore, speak it, Think it into existence! Listed below are some positive daily affirmations for a millionaire mindset.

"Attract Wealth and Abundance".

1. I am always in a State of becoming Greater.
2. I am a magnet for money.
3. Prosperity is drawn to me.
4. Money comes to me in Expected and Unexpected ways.
5. I embrace new avenues of income.
6. I am always in a state of becoming greater.

7. I welcome an unlimited source of wealth and income into my life.

8. I am the master of my wealth.

9. Wealth creates a positive impact in my world.

10. Money comes to me effortlessly.

11. My business is more successful each day.

12. I am connected to the universal supply of money.

13. I attract abundance and prosperity naturally.

14. I have an abundance of Love, Joy and Money in my life.

15. My life is mine to create.

16. I manifest abundance with my unique talents and gifts.

17. I am surrounded by entities who are eager to contribute to my abundance.

18. I accept gifts with appreciation.

19. I forbid thoughts of failure to inhabit my mind.

20. Attracting money is easy.

21. I am becoming wealthy.

22. I am a money magnet.

23. I see abundance everywhere.

24. My income is constantly expanding.

25. I welcome money into my life.

26. I accept financial success.

27. My bank account is constantly increasing.

28. I have the power to attract wealth.

29. My net worth is always increasing.

30. Money flows easily in my life.

31. I am financially free.

32. I create the lifestyle I want.

33. I choose Abundance, Success, Love and Happiness in my life.

34. I honor my worth and value.

35. Money is no longer an issue.

36. I am an excellent money manager.

37. I am an excellent receiver and great giver.

38. I welcome an unlimited source of wealth and income in my life.

39. Money expands my life's opportunities.

40. I attract enough passive income to pay for the lifestyle I want.

41. I get rich doing what I love.

42. I have a positive money mindset.

43. The universe will always serve my best interests.

44. My income is always greater than my expenses.

45. I always have my money coming in than going out.

46. I enjoy managing and investing my money.

47. My prosperity is unlimited.

48. I am worthy of a wealthy life.

49. I add value to other people's lives.

50. The universe will always serve my best interests.

51. I can handle large sums of money.

52. I'm constantly discovering new sources of income.

53. I live each day appreciating value.

54. I see the infinite supply of energy.

55. I am in perfect balance.

56. I am free of worry.

57. I have the power to create change.

58. My wallet bulges with money.

59. I now attune myself to the frequency of money.

60. Everything I do seems to generate more money.

61. I make money in my sleep.

62. My positive attitude towards money attracts abundance in my life.

63. I paid all my bills and still I sit on a pile of cash.

64. Making money is fun.

65. Money seeks me out.

66. I am living a life of Financial Security.

67. I radiate power of attraction.

68. I invite gratitude into my heart.

69. I am a born entrepreneur.

70. I love myself and life

Section 6: Meal Plans

Available in this guide are two types of Meal Plans one for Weight Gain and for Weight Loss. If you are underweight or simply looking to gain more weight, then following high calorie meal option plan can help you reach your goals. This is designed for anyone who is looking to gain weight in a healthy way. This weight

gain meal plan guide will provide you with a balance of healthy and high calorie foods, so you get plenty of nutrients and fiber. 3000 calories would be expected to result in weight gain of 1 to 2 pounds per week depending on gender body size and activity level. Make sure you are combining workout routines with resistance training for muscle building. Accomplishing Weight Loss is easier than you thought. Eating less than you burn is the number one component of weight loss. Turn away from destructive food choices. Build up your self-discipline and make

that change. You must choose to consistently give your body what it needs each day while maintaining a slight calorie deficit if you want to lose weight. Balance out your macros (Protein, Fats, Carbs.) And the way to do that is by learning to eat the right carbs. Plant-based unprocessed foods are so important for losing weight fast and keeping it off. Plant-based foods include high nutrients, it contains no empty calories and it consist of a large quantity of water. Consistently consuming foods that are plant-based and unprocessed will have a profoundly positive impact on your weight loss. Use this Weight Loss Meal Plan option guide to help assist with your weight loss goals. Optional Weight Loss choices include but are not limited to green leafy vegetables like...*Spinach, Kale, Collard Greens, Broccoli, Romaine Lettuce.* Other vegetables choices include...*Tomatoes, Cauliflower, Carrots, Onions.*

Eating a wide variety of fresh fruits is a great source of essential nutrients and antioxidants, here are some examples. *Apples, Grapefruits, Grapes, Melons, Blueberries, Oranges, Strawberries.* Keep a notebook or download certain apps that can track your Macros, Weight and Dates.

Calorie Intake

Besides keeping track of your measurements, you need to calculate your daily average calorie intake. You are required to count calories each and every day and record your totals.

Fitness Pal App is a great way to stay up to date with your calorie intake and much more. To maximize your weight gain, increase the amount of food you are eating with 300-600 calories at a time. Make needed adjustments based on your weekly assessments.

Daily Calorie Allowance Table

Weight	Super Active	Very Active	Active	Moderate Active	Low Active	Sedentary
80	1600	1440	1280	1120	960	800
90	1800	1620	1440	1260	1080	900
100	2000	1800	1600	1400	1200	1000
110	2200	1980	1760	1540	1320	1100
120	2400	2160	1920	1680	1440	1200
130	2600	2340	2080	1820	1560	1300
140	2800	2520	2240	1960	1680	1400
150	3000	2700	2400	2100	1800	1500
160	3200	2880	2560	2240	1920	1600
170	3400	3060	2720	2380	2040	1700
180	3600	3240	2880	2520	2160	1800

The Top 10 Foods Highest in Calories

2000 Calories = 100% DV for Calories

01 Fats and Oils

Calories per Tablespoon (~13g):
- Most Vegetable Oils (124 calories)
- Coconut Oil (121) • Mutton Tallow (117)
- Most Animal Fats (117)
- Butter (100)

02 Nuts and Seeds

Calories per Ounce (28g):
- Macadamias (201 Calories) • Pecans (199%)
- Pine Nuts (188) • Brazil Nuts (184)
- Walnuts (183) • Hazelnuts (181)
- Almonds (162) • Squash Seeds (161)
- Flaxseeds (150) • Chia Seeds (136)

03 Nut and Seed Butters

Calories per Tablespoon (~16g):
- Sunflower Seed Butter (99 calories)
- Almond Butter (98) • Peanut Butter (94)
- Cashew Butter (94) • Tahini (89)

04 Chocolate

Calories per Ounce (28g):
- Dark Chocolate (70-85% Cacao) - 167 Calories
- Dark Chocolate (60-69% Cacao) - 162 Calories
- Chocolate (45-59% Cacao) - 153 Calories

05 Dried Fruit and Fruit Juice

Calories per 1/2 cup (~65g):
- Dried Cherries (266 Calories) • Blueberries (254)
- Prunes (224) • Raisins (217) • Dates (208)
- Apricots (191) • Figs (186) • Apples (104)
- Prune Juice (91) • Grape Juice (76)
- Pineapple Juice (67) • Apple Juice (57)

06 Avocados

- A cup (150g) of Avocado has 240 calories
- An Average Avocado (201g) has 332 calories

07 Whole Grains

Calories per cup (140g):
- Teff (255 Calories) • Amaranth (251)
- Spelt (246) • Kamut (227) • Quinoa (222)
- Brown Rice (218) • Millet (207)
- Barley (193) • Wholewheat Pasta (174)
- Buckwheat (155) • Soba Noodles (113)

08 Milk, Dairy, and Eggs

- Goat's Cheese (75 per oz)•Feta Cheese(74 per oz)
- Whole Milk (149 per cup)
- Ricotta Cheese (108 per 1/4 cup)
- Protein Powder (45 per tablespoon)
- 1 Boiled Egg (78)

09 Oily Fish

Calories per 3oz fillet (85g):
- Mackerel (223 Calories) • Shad (214)
- Herring (213) • Halibut (203) • Salmon (175)
- Trout (162) • Butterfish (159)
- Tuna (156) • Tuna canned in oil (168)
- 3.75oz Can of Sardines (191)

10 Meat

Calories per 3oz fillet (85g):
- Ground Pork (334 Calories) • Turkey Bacon (321)
- Beef Brisket (304) • Lamb Shoulder (303)
- Duck Meat and Skin (286) • Veal (241)
- Chicken Dark Meat (219)
- Chicken Drumstick (173)

Meal Options

8:30am	11:30am	2:30pm	6:30pm		Snack
Water, Egg Whites, or hard boiled egg whites, Oat Brand Flakes Cereal, Turkey Bacon, Whole Wheat Toast, Jam or Peanut Butter, Banana	Protein Bar or Protein Shake, Carrots, Celery & peanut Butter	Rice Bowl, Spinach Salad with grilled Chicken or Tuna. Cheese, Meats, Pasta, Sandwiches, Protein Shake	Baked Potato, Caprese Pasta, Bison, Chicken or Lamb, Asparagus, Broccoli, Crescent or Hawaiian Rolls 5oz White Wine	Protein Shake, Dried Fruits	Italian Ice, Gelato, Ice Cream, Cookies
Water, Protein Shake, Yogurt, Multi Grain Bread/ Bagel, Cinnamon Streusel Muffin, Poached Egg,	Assorted Nuts, Mix Berries- 1Cup, Protein Bar, Avocado Sandwich	Strawberry Feta Salad w/ grilled Chicken, Turkey/ Tuna Melt, Healthy French Fries, Chips Protein Shake	Grilled Chicken w/ Pineapple Salsa, Black Beans Brown Rice, Choice of Meat, Green Beans, Mixed Salad w/ Pine Nuts, Dried Cherries, Kale, Italian	Protein Shake,	2 Boiled Eggs, Greek Yogurt, Granola,
Water, Lox & Cream Cheese on Bagel, Toast, Turkey Bacon, Boiled Egg, Protein Shake	Fresh Berries Vanilla Yogurt/ Smoothie, Granola,	Potato Chips (Lays Original), Ginger Ale, Turkey Sub, Grilled Turkey Reuben, Apple Slices, Protein	Fried Mackerel, French Fries, Hush-puppies, Baked Salmon, Herring, Halibut, Mixed	Protein Shake, Dried Fruits,	Yogurt, Italian Ice, Brownie, Strawberry Shortcake
Water, Banana, English Muffin, Protein Shake, Toast w/ jam, Turkey Sausage, Eggs,	Fruit Platter: Strawberries, Apples, Plums, Blueberries,	Kale/ Strawberry Feta Salad, Peanut Butter & Jelly Sandwich, Veggie Burger, Chips,	Feta Spinach Salad w/ Beef Brisket or Salmon, Dried Cranberries, Almonds, Pine Nuts Baked	Protein Shake	Mixed Nuts, Gelato, Cheesecake, Bananas
Water, Crossant w/ Cheese, Turkey Sausage, Veggie Omelet, Protein Shake	Dried Fruit, Mixed Nuts, Yogurt, Granola Pineapple Juice	Tuna Sandwich, Avocado Egg Salad Sandwich, Cultured Pickles, Boiled Egg, Protein Shake,	Veal, Bison, Duck, Baked Potato, Quinoa, Baked Mac & Cheese, Asparagus, Broccoli, 5oz Red Wine	Protein Shake	Mixed Berry Pie, Gelato, I Ice Cream, Apples
Water, Diced Seasoned Home Potato's, Pancakes, Waffle, French Toast, Turkey Bacon, Protein Shake	Cheese Platter, Fruit Platter, Mixed Nuts	Burrito, Chicken Wrap, Duck Soup, Chicken Soup, Chicken / Fish Tacos, Pizza	Rice & Beans, Grilled Veggie Quesadilla Chicken, Lamb, Baked Sweet Potato, Kale, Boiled Plantain,	Protein Shake, Fruit	Donuts, Pie, Sweet Potato Souffle

Section: 7

Remember we face challenges each day. Don't let negativity or self-doubt stop you from achieving financial success. Create a vision board and write down all the things you would love to manifest along with a schedule to adhere too. Structure and Create your world. Become a Super Entrepreneur with passive income. Build your Personal Website, Sell Videos, Invest in Stocks and Property. All this can be started with just a little bit of Web Camming. If this guide "Somehow" didn't provide you with some piece of information you have a question about, consultations are available and can be scheduled through

Eminence.group@yahoo.com

Keep in mind:

Be Great, Be Entertaining,

Be Consistent, Be a Boss.

Happy Camming!

Appendix

Web Cam Sites:

1. Myfreecams.com pays 50%

2. Streamatemodels.com pays 35%

3. Camsoda.com pays 50%

4. Badgirlent.com pays 50%

Passive Income Clip Sites:

1. https://iwantclips.com/home/model_signup/1a0de4eaaf8 22f1a8be59a8e256dea1a

2. https://www.manyvids.com/Join-MV/164867

**Create your Monthly Subscription Fan club **:

1. https://www.tiffaniloveclub.com/signup

www.ingramcontent.com/pod-product-compliance
Lightning Source LLC
Chambersburg PA
CBHW081643220526

45468CB00009B/2542